AF225722

LESSONS IN BADASSERY

LESSONS IN BADASSERY

HOW TO BREAK ALL THE RULES AND STAND IN YOUR OWN POWER

SHELLY DAVIES

AOTEA

NEW ZEALAND

Aotea Press
Rotorua, New Zealand

Excerpts from *Daring Greatly* and *Listening to Shame* by Brené Brown. Reprinted with permission.

Second Edition

Originally published as *Good Shit I've Learned*, now revised and updated.

Hardcover: 978-0-473-58548-8
Ebook: 978-0-473-58549-5
KDP: 978-0-473-58550-1
Audiobook: 978-0-473-58551-8

Edited by Lauren Taylor Shute Editorial
Cover design by The Book Designers
Cover photography by Photography by Sacha
Interior design by Morgan Krehbiel

TO MY BADASSES-IN-TRAINING: YOU GOT THIS.
AND FUCK, THE WORLD NEEDS YOU.

THE
LESSONS

LESSONS IN BADASSERY

SHALL WE BECOME POWERFUL TOGETHER?

T'S CRAZY TO ME, but somehow, I've become powerful in my world. It's something I notice in small moments, not big ones.

Like the other day when a potential client kept pushing back and sweet-talking me and disrespecting my boundaries when I had declined to take on his project and I replied with one line: "It's a hard no from me."

Powerful.

Like when someone online has an opinion on me or my work or my brand or my way of being in the world. That sounds like a you problem and not a me problem. #bless. #zerofucksgiven.

Powerful.

I think a lot about the concept of power because we tend to think of it hand in hand with control—and that's a bad thing. When we think of powerful people we think of selfish, manipulative dictators, wielding their power.

But me?

I'm powerful in *my* world.

This is me standing in my power. Owning my purpose. Showing up.

I have the power to choose, at any given moment, to act or not to act. To speak or to stay quiet. To go left or go right. To be resistant or be open. To take on a client or not. To charge what I want for my services and expertise. To be generous, to love, to be vulnerable.

And because I KNOW the choices are all mine, I'm powerful.

When people started asking me, how did I become THIS Shelly, the one they see on a stage, owning a room, the one they see facilitating a group of resistant people to completely reframe and reposition themselves, the one who keeps getting up again and again even when life throws her suicidal, addicted, or just plain broken-hearted kids, grandchildren too soon, dead husbands or asshole exes, and ALL THE THINGS, I would answer them:

I dunno, I'm just like everyone else. I've just learned some good shit.

It's taken a long time to fully step into my power, but I think I've found it.
PHOTOGRAPHY BY SACHA

So here you go. A small collection of just some of the good shit that's helped me to learn about and love myself and recognize that the power is in me.

Lessons in badassery, you might say.

Hey, Badass. Shall we become powerful together?

IT'S ALL IN YOUR HEAD

NO, REALLY. All of it. The ability to take control of your life, your emotions, your future, your PAST, it's ALL IN YOUR HEAD. All of it. Life is not about actions—it's about thoughts. Success is not about actions—it's about thoughts. HAPPINESS is not about actions. Say it with me now: it's about thoughts.

So what?

So get therapy. A lot of it.

START NOW.

Here's why.

We think that life is what goes on around us. What we experience, what gets thrown at us, what we do.

It's not.

Life is what happens in our head *in response* to those things. There's literally no correlation between external things and happiness. We all know you can be rich and famous and live in luxury and still be miserable. And we also know you can live a simple, quiet, inexpensive life and still be completely satisfied. You can find joy and beauty in every moment.

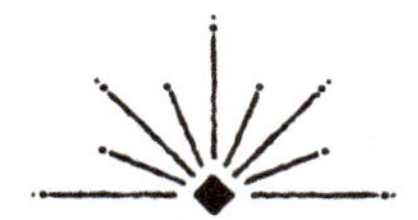

LIFE IS WHAT
HAPPENS IN
OUR HEAD IN
RESPONSE TO
WHAT GOES ON
AROUND YOU.

So, it's ALL. IN. YOUR. HEAD.

That's where therapy comes in.

The more we can learn about the way our brains work, neuro-biologically, cognitively, and psychologically, the more power we have to choose how we respond to any given situation.

By the way, I use the word "therapy" pretty generally. Counseling, coaching, psychotherapy, mentors, wise friends. Take your pick.

Because every human has every resource inside us to be able to thrive, AND I simply don't know of a way to access all those resources alone, we need each other. There is SO MUCH POWER in a skilled outside perspective. Someone to mirror back to us what they're hearing, help us notice faults in our logic, challenge our perceptions and positions.

Wanna know what that looks like in someone's life? Well, take me for example (I mean, duh, that's why you're here). My beautiful Carver Boy (AKA my partner) refers to the old me as demure. I refer to the old me as mousy. Compliant. Definitely forgettable. (Ask anyone who sat next to me in math in high school. Shelly who?)

The old me was afraid to have an unpopular opinion in meetings. The old me didn't know how to respond to being criticised. I'd stay silent then go away and cry.

Me now? After multiple counsellors, three psychologists, a psychiatrist, various coaches, and many, many wise women?

I take no shit.

I give very few fucks.

I've learned to trust my instincts and speak my mind.

I have a voice, and I FUCKING USE IT.

I'm messy and imperfect and always learning, and I'm more than enough.

I show up. Fully, authentically, wholeheartedly.

Those changes have come through taking control of what goes on in my head, and more often than not, some other wise, insightful human has helped me learn how to.

So get therapy. A lot of it.

START NOW.

Wait.

I just wanna make sure you've really processed that.

It's the MOST IMPORTANT THING I'VE EVER LEARNED. If you read nothing else, *read that again*.

IT'S ALL IN YOUR HEAD.

And since it's all in your head? YOU HAVE COMPLETE CONTROL. You. No one else.

If you can't master your thinking, you can't master anything.

Start inside.

Pause everything else you're DOING-—all the external stuff—and go inside. Coz until you're owning that, nothing on the outside is real, and it won't stick.

VULNERABILITY IS STRONGER THAN TITANIUM

THINK I WAS six months or so into my relationship with Carver Boy when he wanted to call it off, *so we don't ruin our friendship.*

Right around that same time, the wisdom of Facebook introduced me to Brené Brown.

Brené Brown's TED talk on vulnerability rocked my world. She was articulating (with evidence to support it) what I KNEW IN MY SOUL and what I already lived in so many ways but had never been fully aware of:

Vulnerability is the root of creativity.

It is the root of connection.

It is the root of our ability to live wholeheartedly.

In her exact words:

> *Vulnerability is the birthplace of love, belonging, joy, courage, empathy, and creativity. It is the source of hope, empathy, accountability, and authenticity. If we want greater clarity in our purpose or deeper and more meaningful spiritual lives, vulnerability is the path.*

That's right—without vulnerability we can't truly love and be loved.

I thought about why Carver Boy was taking this position: he was afraid (like me!) that things would go bad and get messy. After all, things were going great (like, GREAT!) and we'd both lived through plenty of messy. Uggh.

I reflected on the messy I'd lived through. A husband who might have been my soulmate but left me and then died and a sucky marriage that led to an asshole ex-husband and a custody battle. All messy, all miserable, and all over. I'd survived them. I had been battered and bruised but was healed and whole.

So I reflected on the potential risk with my love: I might get my heart broken again.

VULNERABILITY
IS THE EXACT
OPPOSITE OF
WEAKNESS.
IT MAKES US
UNBREAKABLE.

Compare that to the potential benefits: companionship, fulfillment, being seen, understood and accepted, having someone to love and take care of, being taken care of, being able to bring this good man joy.

I announced to him: Yes, this might go badly. I'm willing to take the risk. I can live through a broken heart. *I'll take on that risk for both of us.* I can handle it. I'm all in.

Because, if we break up? That'll suck. But what if we don't?

Where might we be in a year? Two? Ten? How amazing might THAT be?

Bring it.

And just like that, my vulnerability became my strength. My willingness to risk, to be hurt, to experience pain, made me indestructible. Because if I was aware of the possible outcomes and I was willing to accept those, what did I have to lose?

Nothing.

Vulnerability is the exact opposite of weakness. It makes us unbreakable.

PARENTING IS HARD

MY THIRD BABY was six-weeks-old and I was in tears on the phone with my sister, Dione Davies. She's a counsellor and an art therapist, and one of my best friends.

It's so haaaaard, I cried. I suuuuck at this.

For some context: I had a six-week-old, a thirteen-month-old, an eight-year-old, and an unreasonable, zero-emotional-intelligence-gaslighting-husband who did nothing but be demanding and make me feel less-than. We lived on a farm, thirty minutes from anywhere. It was still the days of dial-up internet.

How do you know? She asked.

What do you mean? Her question interrupted my self-pity, just for a moment.

How do you know you suck at it? She asked.

Because no one else is this bad at it, I cried. It's not this hard for everyone else!

How do you know? She asked. (Damn counselling degree.)

BECAUSE I WOULD KNOW! (Cue wailing, tears, and snot. Again.)

HOW would you know?

I WOULD JUST KNOW!!!

I don't remember if she kept talking then or waited for my pity party to play out a little bit longer. But what she said eventually changed everything.

You need to get out. Be with other parents. Find out if what you think is true. Coz it's not. Go to Playcentre, she said.

Playcentre was the closest social activity for people in my demographic, and I was MORALLY AND ETHICALLY OPPOSED TO IT. Playcentre is a bit of an institution in New Zealand—it's been around for eighty years. It's early childhood education with parent involvement, as opposed to day care where you drop your kids and run.

But *Playcentre Mums*. Uggh. They were sooooooo put together and Pollyanna and all-knowing and in control of mothering. I could NOT fit in there. There's no way I'd measure up. I'd be judged, I'd fail, and I'd be miserable every minute.

No way. Nope, No, Na-ah.

crickets

I went.

I mean, what choice did I have? Stay home, alone, miserable and on the edge of sanity? Or give the dumb Playcentre a try and at least have some adult company? I was pretty desperate. Dione was pretty smart. I figured my options were pretty limited, and her advice was the best I had on offer. Dickhead husband certainly wasn't going to help. I called and found out how things worked and when the sessions were.

And the next day I got my son off to school, put the girls in the car, and I went.

And you know what?

Dione was right. (Big sisters often are.)

Cody (5), Grace (3), Me (33), and Lainn (11) in 2007. Parenting was still hard but at least I had dropped the deadweight of a narcissistic husband.
SEDDON PORTRAIT HOUSE

CAN YOU JUST BE A LITTLE BIT KINDER TO YOUR OVERWHELMED, SLEEP-DEPRIVED SELF?

I saw other mums exhausted, struggling, getting up each day and carrying on. I saw them having good days and bad days. On the really rough days they let me sleep on the couch while my kids played with theirs. I learned from their examples, and I felt validated by our mutual struggles.

Parenting IS hard. For everyone.

Duh.

So here's what I want you to know, you beautiful human. If you're a parent, and you're hard on yourself, can you just ease up a little? Can you just be a little bit kinder to your overwhelmed, sleep-deprived self?

The demands of those tiny psychopaths are stabbing you in the brain. Repeatedly. For approximately 21.25 hours of every day. NO ONE can be expected to rise above that with grace and elegance consistently.

Meeting those other mums allowed me to see that I wasn't the only one struggling. It allowed me to change the voice in my head that was telling me, 337 times a day, that I sucked at parenting. It allowed me to reframe: *Parenting is hard. Full stop. I'm doing the best I can each day, and that IS good enough.*

(Shout out to my Playcentre mums Ange King and Sara King. You guys probably have no idea how much you saved my life. Mmmwaaaaah!)

PARENTING IS ESPECIALLY HARD FOR ME

AT SOME STAGE in my late thirties, I started seeing psychologist James Pope. Let's call him *Miraculous James*. I went to see him to work through my ongoing issues with parenting. Not my actual parenting, but how much I still believed I sucked at it. I needed someone else's perspective.

Can I be clear here that I'd been trying to be kind and get rid of my self-judgement about parenting by well over a decade at this stage? Still hadn't nailed that self-judgement. Asshole.

So anyway, Miraculous James asked me if I knew anything about Schema Therapy. (No.) And if I wanted to try it. (Yes. Coz I am *all about the self-awareness.*)

So I filled out a questionnaire—an inventory—a something-or-other. Psychologists love shit like that.

Then we went over it together. It confirmed a lot of things: I'm pretty normal, don't have HUGE hang-ups in terms of self-esteem, I'm neither too much nor too little in most ways.

Way to be middle of the road, Shelly.

But you know where the warning bells went off? UNRELENTING STANDARDS.

I basically expect myself to be the best. Perfect. Constantly achieving. I don't have such high expectations of ANYONE ELSE. Just me. (I guess that's better than being hard on everyone, right?)

It means I punish myself a lot, too. Critique. Judge. I'm very likely to decide I haven't done enough, or good enough, and berate myself for it. Dumb. But that was good to know.

The other two areas I scored highly in were SUBJUGATION and SELF-SACRIFICING. In other words? Putting other people before me. Prioritising their needs over mine. To my own detriment more often than I'd like to admit.

I'M A PEOPLE PLEASER.

If I'm honest, that was *not* a surprise.

I am very driven by wanting people around me to be happy. All the time. Everyone. LIKE IT'S MY JOB. What the ACTUAL fuck.

Then a lightbulb turned on: parenting.

Oh good lord.

IS THIS WHY I THINK I'M THE SUCKIEST PARENT ON THE PLANET?

Ho. Lee. Shit.

Lemme work this through:

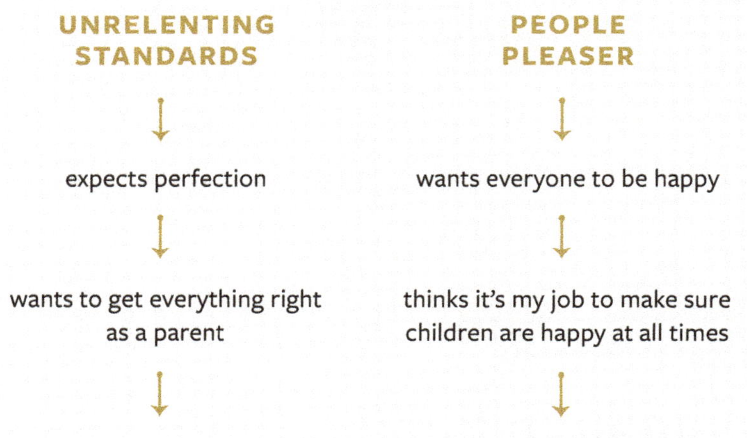

So what we're saying here is, the elements of my personality combine to make THE PERFECT PARENTING NIGHTMARE?

Well shit.

So knowing this doesn't fix it. It doesn't miraculously make parenting any easier. Wouldn't that be niiiice?

What it does do is give me power. Because I can now look at a moment in my parenting, see how I'm feeling, how I'm behaving, and pause and tell myself:

You're feeling guilty because you said no and now the tiny psychopath is sad.

Her sadness hurts your heart. (Mother fucker.)

Being sad won't do her any damage. It'll pass. Letting her be a selfish spoilt brat WILL do her damage. It'll make life hard for her in the long run.

So, your inner-people-pleaser wants to make her happy, and your inner-relenting-standards tell you that her unhappiness is a failure.

They can fuck right off.

As you were.

I gotta say, it's tiring. But it's a hell of a lot more empowering than the self-judgement and shame it leads to.

The good shit I learned here isn't really about parenting though. It's about knowing ourselves. Once I had the tools of understanding some aspects of my personality, then I could look at a situation I was struggling with and use that insight to have power in the moment.

So next time you're struggling in your life, maybe pause and ask:

1. What do I know about myself?
2. How is that playing out in this moment?
3. Is it helping me or getting in my way?
4. What can I do with what I know to change this moment?

Without insight, we don't have power. We're just reacting, existing. I want more than that. Don't you?

HOW OFTEN DO WE WAIT FOR SOMEONE ELSE TO GIVE US PERMISSION, WHEN THE POWER IS ALREADY WITHIN US?

ACT LIKE YOU'RE IN CHARGE, AND YOU ARE

FELT LIKE THE meat in a smelly teenager sandwich. About 200 of them, actually, trying to squeeze simultaneously through a double door into the hall at Opononi Area School. I was the sole Senior English teacher.

Two year 12 boys (doing year 12 for the third time, so coming up on nineteen, only a few years younger than me), rushed up to me.

Miss! Miss! Can we go back to the room?

Why? I asked.

We need to get [insert bullshit excuse I can't remember here].

What I do remember is that, as I was saying No, they both shouted, Thanks, Miss! And made a run for it.

I froze. This was my first year of high school teaching. I had no freaking clue what to do.

Next thing a woman's voice bellowed over me and the fifteen-metres-and-counting-between-me-and-them: OI! YOU TWO! STOP RIGHT NOW!

I couldn't believe it: they stopped.

They turned around. They dropped their shoulders and started skulking back.

Seriously?

I looked to where the voice came from. A lovely petite grey-haired matriarch winked at me and wended her way between the kids. That voice came from her?

She leaned over and said quietly in my ear, just act like you're in charge, and you are. *They can smell fear.*

Then she bellowed again: HURRY UP, YOU TWO!

Well, fuck.

I was twenty-five years old, and that moment had just taught me that to have power, I just had to claim it. For myself. The power was there to be had. The title of teacher gave me the authority, but I had no power unless I claimed it.

How often do we wait for someone else to give us permission, when the power is already within us?

Whose permission are you waiting for?

DON'T EXPECT ONE PERSON TO MEET ALL YOUR EMOTIONAL NEEDS

OK, LOVELIES. Shit's about to get real. What do you get when you cross two failed marriages, a people pleaser, and a bucket full of snot and self-doubt?

Hi, I'm Shelly and I'm a relationship-phobe.

(See what I did there?)

The truth is, after those marriages, I was shit scared. I knew just how twisted a love story could get, how much it can hurt. I knew that when you go all in YA SIMPLY DON'T KNOW.

I literally looked at young couples getting married and I wanted to scream at them:

RUN!

So when things started with Carver Boy, it was NOT a relationship. Don't make me tell you what it was. (Fun. It was fun. Very, very fun. Fuck was it fun.)

By a year in, the blackened charred exterior of my cold dead heart was starting to fall away.

GAHDAMMIT.

I don't know where I found it, but I read some advice from a badass old lady. It was being published because she was 100 or she'd been married for eighty years (maybe both).

She said, you can't expect a single person to meet all of your emotional needs. It's not fair to put all that on them. It's probably not even possible. And she credited that as one of the reasons her marriage had lasted so long.

Smart lady.

I'm pretty sure she mentioned needing to have friends and activities and socialising that didn't include her husband.

Honestly? I'd never thought like that before.

I'd basically had a Disney-fairy-tale-type-romanticism that involved a butt-chin prince who had the magical ability to meet MY EVERY NEED. And I his, I suppose. (Clearly this was before the cold dead heart.)

YOU CAN'T EXPECT A SINGLE PERSON TO MEET ALL OF YOUR EMOTIONAL NEEDS. IT'S NOT FAIR TO PUT ALL THAT ON THEM. IT'S PROBABLY NOT EVEN POSSIBLE.

Apparently, I still thought that's what *the dream relationship* was supposed to be like.

At that time, my life was in flux.

And I was also starting to realize, as I was changing, exploring, and spreading my wings, that I'd created a lot of distance from my previous social networks.

The new me didn't fit comfortably with them anymore.

So it dawned on me, thanks to badass-old-lady-wisdom, that I was relying on Carver Boy for too much emotional support.

Like, all of it.

So I told him that. And I apologised, because it was unfair. And I told him I was going to work on getting some of my emotional needs met through time with peers and girlfriends.

I decided to make more friends.

Oh, look! There you are ❤

See how that worked?

I decided to reach out to people I crossed paths with who were interesting or impressive or who resonated with me. I started being braver and just asking. Want to have coffee? Dinner?

Seven years later, I have an incredible tribe around me. And my emotional reserves get filled by all kinds of people. And the load is lighter for Carver Boy because I'm not putting it all on him. In fact, him meeting my emotional needs is the cream on top. It's the bliss. And what a gift that is to our relationship.

I did that for us. I'm proud of me.

(Oh, and to the WISE GODDESS—AKA Badass Gramma—who I imagine is no longer with us physically—thank you. I've searched. I can't find you. But you know who you are.)

NOT EVERYONE NEEDS A HAND ON THE SMALL OF THEIR BACK

BUT I DO. And we DO all need something.

Figure out what it is you need, and not what the movies tell you you need. What do YOU need so you can be a rock star? Or a unicorn? Or a rainbow-farting-bunny-rabbit?

Me? I needed a hand on the small of my back.

You know, girls, when you walk through a door or climb into a car and your love or your dad or your big brother or some gentleman puts his hand on the small of your back, to support you on your way through?

My Carver Boy taught me how much I needed that, by being that.

To be fully me, to live my truth completely and utterly, to be MORE, I needed the comfort and security and reassurance that someone was right there behind me. And I felt his presence as a gentle hand, with a warmth that radiated through my soul.

I felt it since the first time I drove home from his place in tears, crying my wee heart out because, after eight years on my own, after giving and giving and giving until I simply broke, I had RECEIVED. He

GAVE to me. And let me tell you, that was powerful and universe shattering and changed EVERYTHING.

I don't know what the equivalent to a hand on the small of your back is for you. I don't know what it's like to be you. Maybe a hand on the small of your back will do it for you, too. Maybe you need a cheerleader with pom poms. Maybe you need a couch potato with beers and popcorn.

I don't know what you need but figure it out.

And then get that need met.

And I don't mean sit around crying waiting for someone to show up. Mine is a love story, yes, but the love story isn't what I learned. I'm not suggesting you need to go out and find a lover to fill your empty places (or heal your cold dead heart). What I learned is that I had a need, and once that need was met, I could thrive.

So what I'm suggesting is that you MAKE THINGS HAPPEN so that you can have your needs met.

And first of all, you need to know: What's that need for you?

I don't think there's a single way to figure it out. But some of these will help, I'm sure:

- **Therapy.** Duh. Ask a therapist who knows you well what they see as your greatest emotional needs.
- **Gratitude.** When I note down a few things I'm grateful for each day, themes start arising. I start to see what helps me thrive. What I NEED in my days.
- **Talk** to the people who know you best and longest. Ask them when they can remember you being the happiest, and then dissect what was in your world at that time.
- **Ask** yourself, if I could go back to the best time of my life, when would that be? And then ask, what did I have then that I don't have now?

Once you've identified something you need, start planning ways you can have that need met. And they need to be things you can drive—not things you wait to *happen*. (Like, "I'll have that need met when I find my soulmate." Just NO.)

I need to be clear that that's not what happened for me. I figured out my need because I looked back and reflected on the things that had guaranteed my success, and I saw that the feeling of support was the consistent thing I had through it all.

But in retrospect, I think that if (when) I had figured it out for myself, I could have achieved the same thing—because my potential is IN ME, not in him, the beautiful man with his hand on the small of my back.

Oh, I so love him for that.

But the potential is in me. And it's in you, too.

WHAT I LEARNED
IS THAT I HAD A
NEED, AND ONCE
THAT NEED WAS
MET, I COULD
THRIVE.

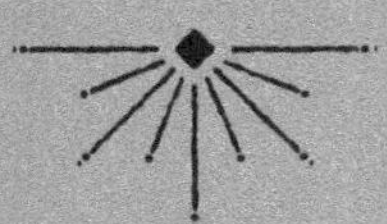

SHAME IS AN ASSHOLE, AND YOU CAN OWN THAT BITCH

MADE A MISTAKE RECENTLY. A big mistake. A potentially career-ending mistake.

Now, I know I'm not perfect. I have ZERO EXPECTATION these days that perfection is even a thing (as much as I love the idea of it). I'm all dancing through life, twirling, and shouting, *I revel in my imperfection!*

(Sounds painful.)

I'm always telling other women—we are amazing and messy and imperfect. AND THAT'S EXACTLY AS IT SHOULD BE!

In fact, I spoke to 100 women about this just two weeks before my big mistake. I was in Shelly Heaven.

But THIS mistake.

This was next level.

I got violent. That was new.

The police were involved. That was new.

You wanna know what happened? You wanna see me walking the vulnerability talk? OK then.

You know those beautiful mum-clashes-with-teenage-daughter moments we all know and love? I found myself in one of those (you can see where this is going, right?). For some reason, on this day, I didn't back down. I didn't apply all the GOOD SHIT I'VE LEARNED and I let myself just go there.

My lovelies, I crossed a line. I lost it. It was a fucking low moment.

I hit my daughter.

And she called the police.

And I was arrested.

And I found myself standing in front of a judge.

AND I FELT SO ASHAMED.

I actually couldn't look people in the eye—that's how ashamed I felt.

I didn't know if I would recover from this mistake. I feared people finding out. It would ruin me. I'd lose all credibility.

SUCH. DEEP. SHAME.

On about day five of this, I turned again to Brené Brown. I knew her vulnerability research had started as shame research. But I had never needed it before.

Well now I did.

And here's what I found. She says:

> *If you put shame in a Petri dish, it needs three things*
> *to grow exponentially: secrecy, silence and judgement.*
> *If you put the same amount of shame in a Petri dish*
> *and douse it with empathy, it can't survive.*

Wait, what? Empathy is the antidote to shame?

HOLY FUCK!

EMPATHY IS ONE OF MY SUPERPOWERS!

(How convenient.)

SHAME IS AN ASSHOLE. DON'T FEED THAT SHIT.

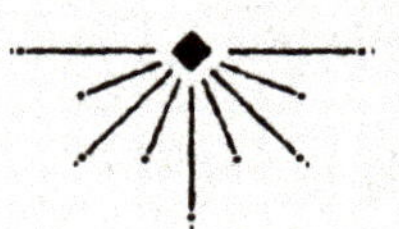

I thought, too, about the secrecy and silence that shame also needs.

And I thought about some of my other strengths: communication and vulnerability.

I knew, in that instant, that I had the ability to overcome this shame. *Everything I needed was in me.*

So I decided:

I will speak my shame.

I will share my story.

I will LOVE AND BE KIND to myself.

The change was INSTANT.

Once I knew what was needed and that I already had it—that was like flicking a switch.

Swish, swish, bish.

Every time someone I trusted asked me how I was doing, I would explain that I'd had a hard time because I hit my daughter and got arrested and charged. I *pushed through* the fear of judgement because I was loving and being kind to myself, reminding myself that I'd had a very human, very public moment, but that's all—just a human moment. And I told them the story because I knew that sharing it would make any shame DISAPPEAR.

And it did.

So I say again: shame is an asshole. Don't feed that shit.

KILL IT (with love, obviously).

CATS ARE ASSHOLES, TOO

THAT IS ALL.

There's nothing you can do about it.

I have it on very good authority that many people agree with me.

Oh, you want the story?

Fine.

I'm allergic to cats. Not deathly-allergic but red-eyes-snot-everywhere-maybe-asthma-attack-allergic.

And after four years with Carver Boy, he was finally ready to move in with me. (Fuck—that was a lesson in patience, let me tell you.)

And here's the thing: Carver Boy came as a package deal with a geriatric cat called Knuckles.

She is, officially, an asshole, and she hates me.

She pees in my suitcases. *When they're packed.*

She tries, every night without fail, to climb up and sleep on my ASS. And every night I kick her off. Repeatedly.

On the rare occasions that Carver Boy is away, she will sit by my head in the middle of the night and randomly SCREECH LIKE SHE'S BEING STABBED.

This is Knuckles, the asshole, in 2020. She's seventeen years old.

ABOVE: how she looks when I take her photo.

LEFT: how she looks when Carver Boy does.

For. Fuck's. Sake.

But you know what? I can live with the asshole cat. I can make that sacrifice for the much, much greater reward: a beautiful man next to me in bed (when she's not wedged in between us, again—FFS) and in life.

So my question to you is this: What can you put up with, to get something better?

What can you sacrifice, if it means a greater reward?

It's a challenging question—because I don't believe we should put up with anything that's doing us *actual harm*. But I do think there are all kinds of things that sometimes we give too much weight to, and they are relatively small things compared to the greater benefit on the line. It's especially true in relationships when we let the empty toilet paper roll or smooshed toothpaste tube get in the way of an otherwise loving relationship.

I'll just leave that question there with you to reflect on.

And as for me? The fucking cat can't live forever, right?

SAY THANK YOU TO COMPLIMENTS

A S A TEENAGER—a PRETTY QUIET TEENAGER, I might add (I know, shut up)—I was seriously lucky to have amazing support around me. Through church, we had weekly activities for youth and classes together as young women.

We learned about our innate value as women. About our sacred roles, our divine heritage, our WORTH.

(Isn't it crazy how I can just talk about that like it's just a thing? Like an everyday thing? No big deal? For me, it just *was*. Don't think I don't realize now how precious that was.)

One particular lesson that has stuck with me was about saying THANK YOU when we were given a compliment.

I don't know if it's the same in all cultures, but in New Zealand that was seen as being pretty *up yourself*. The thing to do instead was to brush a compliment off, run yourself down. Be humble.

But we were told in this lesson that would be pretty rude to the person giving you the compliment, wouldn't it?

I mean, are you accusing them of lying?

SAY NOTHING MORE THAN THANK YOU THE NEXT TIME SOMEONE GIVES YOU A COMPLIMENT.

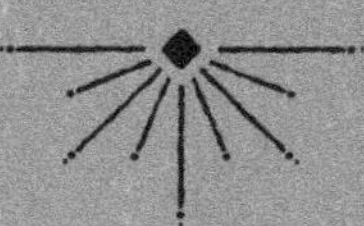

Do you want them to feel stink and stop giving compliments?

So, we were challenged to say nothing more than THANK YOU the next time someone gave us a compliment.

We even practiced it.

Wanna practice it with me?

> *Hey, [insert name here], nice teeth.*
> *Thanks!*

> *Hey, [insert name here], great job on the doodlehorn today.*
> *Thanks!*

See how easy that was?

NERVES AND SELF-CONSCIOUSNESS ARE NOT YOUR FRIEND

YOU KNOW THE BUTTERFLIES, or even worse, the beating drums in your chest when you're about to step onto a stage, or stand up and speak?

Yeah, they bite.

I have the added white-girl-magical-skill of spontaneously turning into a beetroot when I feel self-conscious or nervous.

Yeah, that's fun.

And here's the kicker: I love to sing.

(*I really kind of do wish I was P!nk. Are we surprised?*)

I took singing lessons in my teens and early twenties and learned to control my breathing.

That definitely helped with the nerves. But nerves are only part of it. Self-consciousness is a huge part of it. And what helped with my self-consciousness was a certain level of mastering my SELF-TALK.

I remember a fellow-freckle-queen like me telling me that when we blush bright red, all we can think about is how red we are. We think, red, red, red.

You might not want a photo that looks like this. But without these ones in between? *You don't get the great ones!*
PHOTOGRAPHY BY SACHA

So instead, she said, think blue. Think expansive oceans and icebergs. Think blue, think cool.

In front of a class of high school students, when one darling in the back calls out, Miss, are you pregnant?

(I wasn't.)

Think blue, mother fuckers. Blue.

When I did my first rock star photoshoot in 2016, I went into it knowing there's no way my amazing photographer, Sacha Kahaki, could bring the magic if I didn't give her some good shit to work with.

I am NOT, despite what people think (and what the evidence would suggest) comfortable in front of the camera.

YES, HONESTLY!

And like you, I have a lifetime of photos where I look at them and think, look at that fake smile. Look at how awkward you look. If only you could have just been more relaxed in front of the camera.

So, with money and my brand on the line, I had to give myself a SERIOUS TALKING TO, which went something like this:

Self, I said.

Self.

If you hold back, if you let nerves and self-conscious-ness creep in, it will show.

Self, it's better to go over-the-top and NOT use the photos where you look like a dick than to hold back (so as not to look like a dick) and end up with only average shots.

So, self, be a dick.

Bring it.

The only way you can fuck this up is BY WORRYING ABOUT FUCKING IT UP.

Look, if I'm blunt it's about not giving a fuck (or trying really hard not to).

To BRING IT, whatever IT is, you have to lose the fucks.

Coz caring what people think? That makes you worry.

Worry makes you anxious.

Anxious gives you nerves and makes you smaller.

And none of that shit is going to get you ANYWHERE.

So no matter how scared you get, no matter how much of a dick you might look like, think blue.

(Plus, get an amazing photographer. Love you, Sacha! And do NOT underestimate the power of tequila, music, and your best, potty-mouthed friend at the photoshoot.)

GIVE. THEN GIVE SOME MORE.

MY DEFAULT POSITION IS TO GIVE. It's been built into me, perhaps from a cellular level. It's all I've ever seen, and all I've ever known.

My Great-Great-Grandmother, Tupuna Raihi, instructed her people to clothe, feed, and house the survivors of the shipwrecked SS Wairarapa on our island in 1894. When she was offered a reward by the Union Steam Ship Company, she declined, and instead had them install a telegraph for the benefit of the whole community.

My Grandfather, Tupe (her grandson), was known to never have a coin in his pocket. Because if he saw someone in need, he would give it to them. Even in his eighties, he had a garden big enough to feed a village, and he did. I'm not exaggerating—it was a whole fucking paddock, and no one left his home with an empty stomach or empty hands.

And then there's his son, my dad, who, when he owned a $100,000 car, would loan it to young couples for a weekend so they could have an adventure, and enjoy the luxury.

Seriously. Who even does that?

LEFT: **My exemplar for generosity: Raihi Miraka Te Kewene Davies.**
PHOTO TAKEN CIRCA 1925, PHOTOGRAPHER UNKNOWN.

BELOW: **Gail Davies (Mum), Gordon Davies— Tupe (grandfather), me, Irene Davies (Nana), Robert Davies (Dad) in 1994 at my graduation from Waikato University, Hamilton, New Zealand.**
SYD DAVIES

My mum is service personified. If someone needs, she works to provide what they need. Whereas my dad will buy, she will give time and energy. Sweat.

Mowing the lawns is one of her favourite things. She'll even mow other people's lawns.

So I grew up with those examples and that legacy. That was my normal.

What a thing of beauty.

And before I became #accidentallyawesome, I knew I had writing skills. I mean, the master's degree helped. When people needed something written, I wrote. When they needed an editor, I edited. When they needed a proof-reader, I proof-read.

When I found myself a single mum with only part-time work but full-time bills to pay [insert many swear words here], I decided to try contracting. Freelancing. Whatever you wanna call it.

And here's the magical thing:

ALL THOSE PEOPLE already knew what I could do.

They knew I was a good writer. They knew I was professional and could be relied on. Not only that, but they also felt grateful for my generosity.

So when I needed to start charging for my services? They didn't blink.

It was never an issue.

I was suddenly a professional writer, editor, and proof-reader.

Holy fucksticks.

I truly believe that when we give, it comes back to us.

Have I ever given more than I should? Yes. But do I regret it? No.

Because generosity begets generosity. I've received so much more than I've ever given.

(*Just ask Victor Main who one day gave me his training business. The rest, like I keep saying, is history.*)

HAVE BOUNDARIES

H**I. I'M** S**HELLY**, and I'm a People Pleaser.

Hi, Shelly

I was raised to be generous and kind. To serve. I've always felt that in order to be of worth, I need to be giving.

I based a business on giving generously—to clients, to participants in my training, to people who couldn't afford my services.

I bought groceries for my neighbors, and I felt validated anytime I could rescue someone.

Unhappy? I can help. Hungry? I can help. Lonely? I can help. Not only CAN I help, in fact, but IT'S MY OBLIGATION.

Any red flags in there for you? (Just a few, huh.)

I actually have a very strong belief that my purpose in life is to love. I think it's what I'm HERE TO DO.

So when I watched a very short interview with Brené Brown one day, these words ROCKED ME. She said that in her research, the people she found to be the most compassionate were those with the clearest and most firm boundaries.

What sat with me solidly was that their boundaries were what SUS-TAINED their ability to be compassionate and to love wholeheartedly.

It seemed counterintuitive.

But I could definitely feel the beautiful weight of that concept sitting with me.

And so fuck it, I decided. If I'm so great at loving then I should be able to love myself first, aye?

If I feel it's so vital to be generous (you know: *Give. Then give some more*), I'd better build some boundaries that will safeguard my ability to continue to give. That will ensure I can sustain that generosity.

What do my boundaries look like? They shift. But at the highest level, they're based on these questions:

Do I have the time/energy/headspace/funds to give here?

Will giving do me any harm?

Will giving put my family at a disadvantage? Am I stealing from them?

If this person/group receives my gift in any spirit other than the generous and unconditional spirit in which I gave it, what risk is posed to me? Can I handle the potential outcomes? *What's the worst that can happen?*

BOUNDARIES, PROTECTIONS, LINES TO DRAW WHERE THE YES BECOMES NO—THOSE FREE ME.

It was such a huge learning moment. Boundaries, protections, lines to draw where the YES becomes NO—those free me.

Surprisingly, once I became clear about my own boundaries, it wasn't overly difficult to assert them. The hardest part of the process was me getting clarity, establishing them, committing to them. I had to play through how people might respond to me asserting my boundaries and be prepared for those outcomes. After that, the words came easily.

When my teenager calls, hoping for a ride home from school because it's raining, and I've just sat down for coffee with a friend?

> *Oh, that sucks. Dumb. Hey, I've gotta get back to my meeting now. Love you!*

When a client wants me to drop everything and do something for them now?

> *I can schedule that for Wednesday.*

When I'm invited to take up a governance role that's not right for me at the moment?

> *I won't be able to give that role the commitment it needs right now.*

Prepare some phrases for when you need to say no or pushback. Keep them in your pocket. It's incredibly hard to pull them out of thin air in the moment. But if you're prepared, you're dangerous. In all the best ways.

She's a smart lady, that Brené Brown.

SUPERPOWERS AND KRYPTONITE

SPENT MOST OF MY LIFE believing I was too sensitive, naïve, and a bit flighty.

I thought, as I got older, that I needed to work on becoming tougher, less rose-coloured-glasses, and more disciplined. Those were the pathways to personal growth. Or so I thought.

I'd been running my business for about four years when I had an opportunity to use a tool called CliftonStrengths.

Now, I gotta tell ya that I LOVE all the psychometric tests and personality profiling things around. Myers Briggs, DISC, squiggles and squares, water, air, fire, coloured dots. You name it, I've looked into it.

I also know many of these are considered flawed and junk science. IDGAF. Because I don't consider any of them to be 100% truth. I consider all of them as potentially giving me valuable insights into who I am, what drives me, how I work. And for me, knowing that is POWER.

I also take what I want from each of these tools and disregard what doesn't feel true for me. I'm selective.

Having said all that, though, CliftonStrengths is my favourite. It's SO SIMPLE to understand and I've always found it to be spot on. It's a tool that helped Carver Boy truly understand some of our differences, and gave him the vocab so we could discuss those differences.

So I took the test and it told me that three of my greatest strengths are:

Empathy, positivity, and adaptability.

I HAD NO IDEA THOSE WERE STRENGTHS!

Empathy? I thought I was overly sensitive. Quick to cry.

Positivity? I thought I was naïve—that I ignore warning signs. (That's what another personality profile had told me. Assholes. Plus, see my second marriage).

Adaptability? I thought I was flighty, all over the place, disorganized, can't stick to a plan.

The short story? Three things I thought were *faults in my character* are actually my SUPERPOWERS. That changed everything.

The reframe triggered a rebrand. The new brand leveraged off those strengths:

I TRUSTED my ability to relate to my readers/clients' context and speak to them empathetically. So my voice got stronger. Less hesitant. Less apologetic. More confident.

Instead of feeling like I needed to hold back on my bounciness and enthusiasm and optimism, I WENT ALL IN. I made sure every word in my marketing oozed positivity.

Since I now knew I was adaptable and that was a good thing, I could now LEVERAGE that with my clients. I could give them the reassurance that whatever gets thrown at me, I can get us to our destination.

Reframing what I thought was my kryptonite into my superpowers was a significant point in my growth.

Like I said at the very beginning: It's all in your head.

Weakness or strength?

Well, now that just depends how you look at it.

THREE THINGS I THOUGHT WERE FAULTS IN MY CHARACTER ARE ACTUALLY MY SUPERPOWERS.

YOU DON'T NEED PERMISSION TO LEAD

ONCE HAD an amazing boss named Kate Cherrington. In only eighteen months, with her as my example, I learned almost everything I know about being a leader.

When she built her team, she hired us firstly because of *who we were* and after that, what we could do. She *saw* us. She knew our abilities and our potential.

And then she put us to work. With complete trust that how we chose to do it was the best way. And that we would do it.

And, at the same time, she was right there at our backs, whenever we needed her. She DIDN'T throw us in the deep end and leave us to flounder and hope for the best. She placed us where she saw we could add value, gave us the mandate and resources to do what was needed, expressed absolute faith in our abilities to do it, and stayed close but not too close.

With someone believing in me like that, how could I not?

So, when Kate inserted me into a working group or onto a project, saying, Shelly can write that resource for you, or Shelly can facilitate that process for you, I believed her. I mean, she was a wise, loving, generous, influential woman. She was easy to believe.

I figured I must be up to the task.

One of the reasons she was easy to believe (and trust so completely) was because she was always willing to *take one for the greater good*. It was like she had no ego—or if she did, she never let it show.

She "gifted" our team members to lots of initiatives throughout the organisation. What an amazing way to influence! We were GIFTS—valued contributions to benefit the project—how does someone refuse that? She gifted us strategically so we could influence and make sure things were aligned. She kept a finger on the pulse of all of it.

So here's the kicker. Here's what makes her my hero.

When someone in one of those many initiatives dropped a ball, inevitably people involved would start to point fingers.

Kate would jump into the conversation and say, Oh sorry guys, my bad. And just like that, with someone taking responsibility, the conflict was resolved. The project could get back on track.

She was never the one in the wrong.

But she took the blame. Because that was how everyone could get back to focusing on the bigger, better picture: achieving good outcomes.

I barely have words to describe what kind of person is willing to put themselves on the line like that, because she knew full well it wasn't about her. It was never about her. It was bigger.

She also taught us to *transgress*.

A transgression is when you break a rule for a greater good. It's when breaking a rule doesn't mean you're doing anything ethically or morally wrong, but there IS a rule, and you transgress it. Because it's what's needed to get a good outcome.

I JUST TRUST
THAT WHEN
I KNOW
SOMETHING
IS RIGHT AND
GOOD, I HAVE
THE ABSOLUTE
RIGHT TO ACT
ON IT.

For me, little-miss-goodie-two-shoes, never having broken rules my entire life because I was shit scared of getting in trouble, this was terrifying.

And exhilarating.

And emancipatory!

She taught us that we didn't need permission to do what's right. Not ever. Not anywhere. She called it self-leadership, and it was something I'd never considered before.

At an event (not even our event, just some random event), if something had been overlooked, she taught us to just go ahead and fix it.

Take initiative.

Give ourselves permission to take on that responsibility rather than sit quietly feeling uncomfortable and thinking, *They should be doing X. Why won't they just do X?*

Just fucking get up and do X.

You do it.

And Kate led by example. Diplomatically, humbly, gently wending her way through each day doing what's right without harming anyone, and also without asking permission.

What an example. What a privilege. I practice self-leadership like this now (on a good day). It's one of the things that makes people think I'm something special—that I'm not afraid to step up and do what needs to be done, without permission or someone asking me to.

I'm not special, I just trust that when I know something is right and good, I have the absolute right to act on it.

Those eighteen months changed my life.

(You can tell how serious I am about this, coz I couldn't even get cheeky in this whole chapter. Kate Cherrington is my fucking hero.)

YOU ARE DESCENDED OF DIVINITY

Was raised to believe that I had earthly parents and heavenly parents.

That is, Mum and Dad, plus a Heavenly Mother and a Heavenly Father. That meant that all people were created in spirit first, then our earthly parents gave us a body.

I can't give you a starting point to this story because it was literally all I knew, all my life.

I have questions about religion these days.

But what I don't doubt is that as humans we have a heritage that is greater than THIS. Greater than the here and now, the observable, the tangible.

I believe there is divinity in us.

And if that's your starting point then a couple of things happen:

1. You're generally going to be good to other humans, and
2. You have to acknowledge that you're worth something.

If we all believed there was divinity in every being, what would that change?

Would it change how we give? Serve? Love?

Would it change how we hold grudges or forgive?

Would it change how we judge, criticize, or seek to understand?

Would it change how we treat ourselves? How we talk to ourselves?

I know so many amazing humans who say awful things to themselves: They call themselves stupid. Dumb. A loser. They say *I'm no good at X.*

They'd never say that to other people.

I hope that we all start to recognize the divine heritage and potential in all of us and start treating ourselves accordingly.

Love you. (That's an order.)

IF WE ALL BELIEVED THERE WAS DIVINITY IN EVERY BEING, WHAT WOULD THAT CHANGE?

WHAT'S THE WORST THAT COULD HAPPEN?

WAS GOING THROUGH divorce number two, and unlike number one which was fast and relatively simple (on the outside), this one was messy all over.

Drawn out.

Complicated.

Filled with guilt and manipulation and fear and insecurity.

I wasn't coping, so I decided to try a psychologist. I found Jo Clarkson, AKA *Lifesaver Jo*.

Lifesaver Jo had a little whiteboard and as she talked, she'd draw diagrams.

I learned MANY THINGS from her.

I learned about ruminating. Which freaked me out to be honest, coz I learned in primary school that that's what cows do, chewing their cud. Ruminant animals.

Um, yeah.

Not a cow

Um, Yeah.   LAUREN TAYLOR SHUTE

But I was ruminating. Going over and over and over scenarios in my mind that I wanted to fix. If I just had this conversation. If I just said that. If I could just make him understand X.

I was chewing on that shit day and night. Uggh.

Ruminating is NOT COOL. And it's a bugger to fix. But with Life-saver Jo, I learned some tools.

They're not miraculous, and the very nature of ruminating is that it happens when we don't notice, so the tools are about noticing so we can take control of our thoughts. Tools like:

* **Mindfulness**—Learning to stop and become aware of my thoughts was the first step. Stop groaning. It's an actual thing, and it actually is necessary for our sanity.

- **Distraction**—Simply pointing my brain at a different topic can help: Let's plan what we're going to do when we get out of the shower. Once I park the car, what's next?
- **Interruption**—A process of interrupting the rumination cycle by asking questions like: And then what? So what? And what then?

One question I learned to ask as a way of interrupting the cycle, was, *What's the worst that can happen?*

This question has been my go-to ever since.

Like, if I don't answer this text from my emotionally abusive ex-husband, what's the worst that could happen?

He'd be angry.

And will he act on that? Are you in danger?

No.

Then can you live with that possibility?

Yes. Fuck yes.

Does it actually matter to you whether he's angry or happy or sad? Do you care?

No.

Is it your job to keep him happy? Is that your responsibility?

Fuck no.

Well then what are you going to do?

Not fucking answer that text, that's what.

BOOM.

It's called catastrophizing. When you need to make a decision, play out the worst possible outcomes. Ask yourself if you'd survive if the worst happened.

I am my absolute most powerful when I've prepared myself with this thought process. It removes fear by making me aware of any risks, and giving me the chance to decide, ahead of time, whether that's something I'm prepared to live with.

Once fear is acknowledged and mitigated, I can act with confidence. Every. Time.

Can I carry that level of risk?

If the answer is yes, DO IT.

There's a reason you want to.

Don't let *what if*s stop you.

YOU CAN BE A GOOD PERSON AND BE WEALTHY

IKE, DUH, RIGHT?

But no, not duh, coz I didn't realize that.

When I started my business, I was intensely uncomfortable with what I was charging clients. So much so, in fact, that over the first two or three years, I slowly undermined my own prices.

Here's an example.

I started with a training day rate of $3,000. It was a rate I inherited with the beginnings of the business, and it felt pretty obscene.

So when a new client came to me, I'd say, well my usual day rate is $3,000, but if that's a problem, I'm always happy to negotiate. (Good Lord. I was so *nice*.)

Eventually, I was charging half of my clients only $1,000–$1,500 for a day of training.

That's just dumb.

So what did I do? Therapy. (Surprise!)

Meet Lynda Moore, Money Mentalist.

She took me through a whole process of figuring out my money story and my core beliefs and values around money. Yet again—awareness is the basis of change.

The BIGGEST breakthrough for me was discovering that deeeeep down, I thought you had to make a choice. I believed you could either be a GOOD PERSON, or a WEALTHY PERSON. The end. Pick one.

THAT'S RIDICULOUS! But there it was, hiding in the depths (of my cold, dead heart).

I didn't think money was inherently evil, but I did think there was something immoral in chasing after it. In wanting wealth. I was morally opposed to being *all about the money.*

Honestly, awareness was all it took. That flipped a switch. Because I knew, intellectually, that it was simply NOT TRUE. I could list a bunch of people I know personally who are deeply good, kind, loving, generous people, and also are financially very well-off. So I had evidence.

And I also had a reframe:

> *I can be a good person AND seek after financial security.*

> *The two are NOT mutually exclusive.*

> *I can be good and kind and generous and still place financial value on my skills.*

I can be both!

In fact, being financially secure gives me options. I can be more generous when I'm financially secure, comfortable, and charging what I'm worth and what businesses are willing to pay is how I'll get there.

I mean come on... At the very least, I can seek financial security for my kids. DUH.

FUCK IS NOT A DIRTY WORD

UNLESS YOU MAKE IT ONE. In fact, nothing is a bad word unless you decide it is.

For thirty-eight years, I didn't swear. I was a good religious girl, and there were LOTS of things I just wouldn't dream of doing. Saying *fuck* out loud was one of them. Although I did *think* it. And there was that one time I told my second ex-husband to shut-the-fuck-up, but he deserved it. And I was kind of proud of myself. And probably repented afterwards.

Anyway, so at thirty-eight, when I left church and spread my wings and started drinking coffee and alcohol and sleeping with a man I wasn't married to (gasp), I also started swearing. Eventually.

I was INCREDIBLY self-conscious about saying fuck out loud. I'm not sure what I thought would happen. Lightning maybe?

But I wanted to be the same on the outside as I am on the inside, so I pushed through.

Apparently, I've mastered the art of profanity. And I'm proud of it.

I think about it a lot, because people have all kinds of sensitivities and judgements about swearing. And I'm good with that. Coz my people? They swear, or they don't mind me swearing. If you're in any other camp, probably not my people. Easy aye?

Coz here's the thing. Nothing is offensive unless you decide it is. No one can actually offend you. Only you can choose to be offended.

Do you hear that? Next time you hear the words *you make me feel...* coming out of your mouth, MEEEHP, WRONG!

You CHOOSE to feel that way in response to what someone says or does or doesn't say or do.

Own your choices, own your feelings. Own your language.

Know that there are consequences of choosing to say *fuck* and be willing to accept them.

Or don't say *fuck*.

(The whole choose how you feel thing came from a Psychologist. Probably Lifesaver Jo. But it was the stunningly-high-class and potty-mouthed Belinda Thomas who taught me how to say fuck. Epic.)

KNOW THAT THERE ARE CONSEQUENCES OF CHOOSING TO SAY FUCK AND BE WILLING TO ACCEPT THEM.

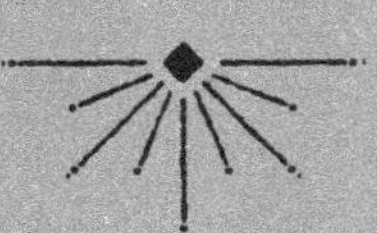

SHOULDS ARE ROGUE PREFERENCES

I remember hearing many wise women at various times in my life talk about removing the SHOULDs from our lives. About how they weigh us down. They put pressure on us. We punish ourselves over what we're not doing (or being) but think we SHOULD.

I probably took that thinking on to some extent.

But I found myself in a session with Miraculous James talking about how I SHOULD do a bunch of things. I was feeling completely overwhelmed (a very regular occurrence), and I was swimming in SHOULDs.

First of all, I wrote out all the SHOULDs. Got the noise out of my brain and in front of me where I could work with it.

Miraculous James explained to me how SHOULDs are just preferences that we've given too much weight. Too much power. They're runaway preferences.

ROGUE PREFERENCES!!

It goes like this, he said:

1. **DEMAND**—*Life SHOULD be like THIS. But it's not. So,*
2. **AWFULISE**—*It's all terrible, it's too much. So,*
3. **IMPOSSIBLE**—*I can't cope. And since I can't cope,*
4. **LABEL**—*I'm not good enough, I'm a failure, I'm not worthy.*

(Well that down-spiralled pretty quickly, aye? Fuck!)

Instead, we can reframe it like this:

1. **PREFERENCE**—*I'd prefer it if life was like this. But it's not, and,*
2. **UNPLEASANT**—*That sucks. But,*
3. **POSSIBLE**—*That's OK. That's just life. I can cope with that. And since I can cope,*
4. **HUMAN**—*I'm just a human being. Like everyone else. And I'm doing fine.*

This was a thought pattern I was completely unaware of.

BEING MALLEABLE IS A MUCH MORE PLEASANT EXPERIENCE THAN BEING A THING THAT CAN SHATTER.

Do you hear that, y'all? How a simple SHOULD leads us to self-loathing and punishment and reinforcing our beliefs that we're not enough?

PLEASE, read it again.

Think of one of your *shoulds*.

Run it through the original thought process (you know, the one that crashes and burns like a mofo).

Now run it through the reframed thinking.

SEE HOW THAT WORKS?

HEAR HOW FREAKING EXCITED I AM FOR US?

Don't let your preferences go ROGUE. They are only preferences. They aren't everything. They're malleable.

So are you.

And trust me, being malleable is a much more pleasant experience than being a thing that can shatter. No one's got that much glue.

(By the way, I'm claiming the term Rogue Preferences. James might be miraculous, but I have some miracles in me, too.)

DO YOU ENJOY IT?

OK, THIS ONE'S FRESH. Like, last week, fresh.

In my career, I've gone from lazy-ass-employee (really convinced I was lazy like 80% of the time) to CRAZY-DRIVEN-NON-STOP-MANIC-PUSH-TILL-I-BREAK self-employed chicky.

In the latter phase, I've strived for balance. That fucking work-life-balance bullshit everyone talks about and that I don't subscribe to, but I still knew there was something not right if I was falling into bed on the verge of tears or in a drunken stupor each night.

I was on a podcast call with Christina Marlett of Courageous Self-Care. I said to her that in terms of my THINKING—my self-talk and my resourceful ways of thinking—I'm great with self-care. But in terms of my day-to-day workload, scheduling, the practicality, the logistics, I still hadn't got it right. I explained that I spend way too much time feeling manic and breathless and rushing, always rushing, pushing, and arriving late to something, YET AGAIN. Never mind that my idea of late is three minutes...

And she asked, *But do you enjoy it?*

BACK THE TRUCK UP!

Do I enjoy it? FUCK YES, I DO!

Good Lord, are you serious? Is that all I need to do? Realize that when I'm manic and frantic, I'm in my zone? That's my flow state? I THRIVE on that?

Coz I do. AND there needs to be an end to it—I can't exist like that always. So as long as there's an end to it, as long as at some-thing-o'clock-pm I switch off and snuggle on the couch and have a glass of something delish, I can just spend all that time going, WOOHOOOO! I'M ON A RIDE AND I'M LOVING IIIIIIITTTT!!!

So when I got back from a beautiful break in Tahiti and had to get up at stupid o'clock and write like a maniac for a client deadline in between meetings and phone calls and THERAPY and office hours, and I didn't get to stop until sixteen hours later, I smiled, I revelled, I congratulated myself.

And when I had to spend THE VERY NEXT DAY working and having meetings instead of *recovery day* like my calendar said (and says every Friday, and I routinely ignore), I revelled in the fact that those were meetings I was voluntarily having, because I WANTED TO. Because they were with great people and involved winter sunshine and crisp air and drunk whiteboard brainstorm sessions. Because I was being creative and fulfilled and LOVING LIFE.

I just wasn't napping like I'd like to in a parallel universe. Or like I think I should (and I should. Sometimes. Fucking rogue preferences).

I always would have enjoyed those two manic days straight off the romantic Tahitian getaway. AND I would have had a constant inner critic saying, *But you should be managing this better. You need bal-ance. You're still not getting it right. You should know better than to push yourself this hard.*

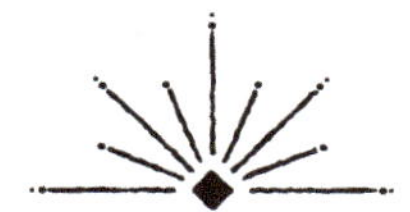

IF YOU ENJOY YOUR FLOW, AND IT'S WORKING, AND IT'S NOT CAUSING ANY HARM, THEN IT'S NOT A PROBLEM.

I reframed. I changed that voice. I went internal and OWNED THAT SHIT. And HELLO! Satisfaction levels? Through the roof. Day-amn, Christina Marlett! Where have you been all my life!

So, when are you in your zone?

What does your flow state look like?

And now when you're in it, are you bringing guilt and SHOULDs with you?

Maybe just check.

Coz if you enjoy it, and it's working, and it's not causing any harm…? Then it's not a problem, is it.

I CAN DO GRIEF

WE HAD A nasty family court battle going on over my first grandson. Yes, grandson. I was forty when my seventeen-year-old son started procreating, little douchebag.

The other grandparents had decided I was A) dishonest, B) not able to love our grandson as much as they did, and C) just generally not a capable caregiver.

I felt sick in my stomach. I felt anxious. I was ruminating.

I saw Miraculous James.

Apparently, his miracles were on hiatus, because it didn't help.

I did all the things I knew to do to manage anxiety.

They didn't help, either. I was walking around with rocks in my gut.

I saw James again—WHERE ARE YOUR FUCKING MIRACLES?

I was freaking out. Anxiety was not something I'd ever had real problems with. I'm pretty good at the whole CBT (Cognitive Behavioural Therapy) thing, recognizing my thoughts, and changing them, to change my reality.

KNOWING MAKES YOU POWERFUL.

When I had occasionally had some anxiety, I'd always been able to talk myself through it.

WHY WASN'T IT WORKING THIS TIME???

As we talked, we realized that it was not anxiety I was feeling.

It was grief.

The sick feeling was loss. It was loss of the life I'd wanted for my son with his children. It was loss of the relationship I'd hoped to have with the other grandparents. It was loss of some freedom now that I was going to need to take more responsibility for this beautiful grandson than I'd have preferred to.

I was grieving.

And knowing that changed EVERYTHING.

Because grief? I know how that goes. I've survived it before. I knew to ride the wave, not deny it, and eventually it would lessen. It would become something liveable.

And it did. *pokes her tongue out*

I can do grief. I know how to live it, experience it, survive it.

Knowing that was powerful.

What can YOU do?

Because the good shit I learned here isn't actually about grief or anxiety. It's about the power of knowing what we CAN DO. What can you live through, navigate, cope with, overcome?

Knowing makes you powerful.

Once I recognized that what I was experiencing was grief, and I'm 100% sure I can DO grief, then I was no longer afraid and treading water within what was going on. I felt capable. Grief doesn't scare me.

I've lived through the love of my life breaking my heart then drowning. I've lived through identifying his body when it had been in the ocean for three days. I've lived through a second, shitty marriage, and the feelings of failure when I ended it.

I've grieved, and I've survived.
I can DO grief.

What do you KNOW FOR SURE you can do?

Is it hard work?

Because if it's hard work, then when you realize that the epic mountain ahead of you is scalable as long as you just keep putting one foot in front of the other, you can just brush away fear and go, I got this. Me and hard work.

Is it patience?

Because if it's patience, then when you realize in a hard situation that waiting it out is likely to be your best option, you can just chill the fuck out, and go, OK then, I'll wait. I can do patience.

Is it having hard conversations?

Because if it's having hard conversations, then when everyone else at work is skirting around the elephant in the room, you can just go, Hey, I can do hard conversations, and without fear you can address the problem.

Maybe just stop right now and acknowledge one thing you KNOW you can DO. And next time you're scared, overwhelmed, out of control, maybe even hopeless, ask yourself if that THING that you know how to do can help.

You got this.

THERE'S ALWAYS GOING TO BE ANOTHER *THING*

'M GOING TO take credit for this one. Yup, I figured something out all by myself. Surprising, I know! (Shut up.)

I was in the middle of *something*. Some drama. Honestly, it could have been anything, because there's always something. (When I reminded Miraculous James about it recently, he said, *Oh, yeah, I remember when you figured that out... Something was going on. I can't remember what it was. But it was something GNARLY.* And then we both cracked up. Sigh. Yup, this is my life.)

So there was some big thing I was struggling with. My young teenage daughter had made a decision that broke me. Or my teenage son had knocked up his girlfriend. Again. Or we were in the middle of a custody battle. Or a rehab journey. Or *something*—you get the picture.

And I realized that during each of these things I held on by the skin of my teeth, I white-knuckled it, and just waited until it passed, looking forward to the peace on the other side. To the time when the drama would be finished. *When life would go back to normal.*

Can you see where we're heading with this?

I was like, Oh fuck.

DUH.

There is no peace! There is no normal. There is no *getting through this* and coming out the other side. On the other side will be:

The. Next. Thing.

I figured this one out all on my own.

There's always a next thing! I mean, seriously. For me it tends to be parenting, but not always. The next thing might be cancer. Or unemployment. Or financial stress. Or bad neighbours. Or a crime. Or a natural disaster. Or a pandemic, FFS. I'm not trying to be pessimistic here, but in my experience, *there is always a next thing*.

So I decided to reframe.

> *Right now, I'm dealing with _______. I'll get through it. And after this, there will be a next thing. Because that's how life works. And that's OK, coz look at all the things you've survived so far. Look at all the evidence that this, too, will pass, and YOU'LL STILL BE STANDING AT THE END OF IT.*

You might be reading this and going, DUH, Shelly. Like, slow learner.
But this was HUGE for me.
And it meant I moved from a constant state of—

> *Life is hard and this awful thing's going on and I can't
> wait for it to be over.*

to—

> *I'm dealing with this hard thing, and I'll be OK, and
> this is what life is like.*

I almost started to wonder what the next challenge might be.
gulp
Don't wait for this *thing* to end so that you can be happy. Find the
happy alongside of the thing. Or while you sit in the thing. While you
ride the thing out.
Or you really might never be happy.
And THAT, my loves, would be a tragedy.

YOU DON'T HAVE TO BE EVERYONE'S CUP OF TEA

MEAN, FUCK. I don't even like tea.

Erika Napoletano taught me this one.

I'd been developing my brand over the years, and it was going well. I had rebranded myself under my name, because I'd realized it was me my clients wanted. I felt confident. Business was good.

The website I had was aimed at the corporate market. It was already a bit more personal and less conservative than my digital marketing guys thought I should be, because I was learning that I am my brand. But it was also a watered-down version of A) who my clients got in person, and B) who I really wanted to be, all the time.

This is what we do with brand. We're afraid to offend. We create a brand, write our copy, run it by people we know and trust, and because they care, they advise caution.

Oh, maybe you shouldn't say this. And maybe soften that.

They mean well. They don't want us to get hurt, fail. They encourage us to be conservative because it feels safer.

Even brand agencies do this. Grrrr.

THE MORE
YOU SPEAK TO
YOUR TRIBE,
THE MORE
SUPPORT YOU
HAVE TO BE
YOU ALL THE
WAY.

So my friend Sally Stephenson, a fellow writer and badass businesswoman, told me about Erika Napoletano.

I jumped onto her website.

I. Could not. Believe. My eyes!

She had pictures of her that were so honest. So personal. Laughing. Silliness. Lots of them.

And SHE SWORE.

She was ballsy and gutsy and everything I was inside but didn't think I could be on the outside.

She said, and I'm paraphrasing here, you only need a loyal tribe. People who get you. And the stronger you speak to your tribe, without worrying about offending others, the more your tribe will be drawn to you and the more others will fuck off.

The more you speak to your tribe the more support you have to be you all the way.

Well, fucknugget.

There's been no turning back.

What's something you hold back on, for fear of offending or upsetting someone? What would happen if you brought that thing into one more aspect of your life?

Test it out. You don't have to go all in (I kept a complete backup of my previous website in case I needed to unfuck my business after the rebrand, LOL).

Baby steps. Be more you in one place. See what happens. Know that SOME people might not like it.

Do those people matter? Do you need to give their opinions weight?

You don't have to be everyone's cup of tea. You could be their two shots of vodka (glug, glug, glug…).

I CAN LIVE THROUGH EVEN THE BIGGEST FAILURES

N 2018, I HAD a psychologist tell me, TO MY FACE, that the reason my twenty-one-year-old son was struggling in his life was because I had never been able to provide him with the safety and security he needed as a child.

WHAT THE ACTUAL FUCK.

Yup, you heard it right.

You know the absolute, bare minimum, most basic requirement of even vaguely decent parenting? Giving your child a safe environment? Yeah that.

I HAD FAILED.

To give this some context, I had done a couple of years with Life-saver Jo developing some tools and then three years with Miraculous James FINALLY reaching a point where I was starting to believe I had done a half-decent job as a mother. I had stopped calling myself a failure as a parent. I had started being generous to myself and looking at my beautiful children as evidence that I wasn't a complete failure.

And now this.

Now, before you get all up in arms and defensive about what this VERY EXPERIENCED OTHER PSYCHOLOGIST said (because all my ninja cheerleaders do, and I love you for that), some more context:

I had asked her to do a full psychological assessment of my son. I was worried about him. She was giving me her professional opinion on HIS life experience and how it had shaped him. She wasn't critiquing me. In fact, I imagine she felt fairly uncomfortable stating it to me that plainly. I respect her for that.

I went home, got drunk, and woke up the next morning crying. I cried for three days. Maybe four.

On one of those days, I was literally foetal on the floor of the shower, sobbing. It was possibly the most intense emotional pain I've ever felt.

YOU CAN CARRY FAILURES HEAVILY, AS BAGGAGE, OR YOU CAN USE THEM AS STEPS THAT YOU CLIMB, RISING EVER HIGHER AND HIGHER ABOVE THEM.

I had recently stopped seeing Miraculous James because everything was going well. *Insert hysterical laughter here*

I texted him. When can you fit me in? This one's a doozy.

And as always, Miraculous James delivered.

Here's basically what he convinced me, so I could repeat this to myself as often as I needed to:

1. Humans are messy.
2. Everyone's messy is different.
3. Some of our messes are more visible than others.
4. I happened to have recently had one of my messes brought excruciatingly to the foreground.
5. Given my own trauma with a dead husband, depression, a bad marriage, more depression, and single parenthood, I had given him the absolute best I was capable of.
6. My absolute best REALLY wasn't too shabby.
7. BUT! Some chimpanzee babies just have ridiculously high levels of emotional need. (There's some research on this, apparently. But I don't know where it is.)
8. Some chimpanzee babies get paired with a magical-unicorn-of-a-chimpanzee-mother, and they do OK.
9. The rest of those chimpanzee babies just get fucked up. It's not because they have bad mothers. It's just one of those things.
10. Did I mention humans are messy?

So, yeah. This felt like a big fucking failure. Even with all the good thinking around it, it still really hurt.

AND I survived it.

Hello world? Come at me. What else ya got?

Look back at what the world has thrown at you.

Still standing? Yeah, you are.

In 2019, my son and I are closer than ever.

And you can carry those things heavily, as baggage, or you can use them as steps that you climb, rising ever higher and higher above them.

So, heeeeey, warrior woman!

There you are.

I see you.

When you can take stock of what you've survived, and recognize that you're still standing, you can KNOW that you're ready for the next mother fucking thing that's coming. No fear. Just self-love and power.

And that, my friend, is badassery at its finest.

GETTING OLDER ROCKS!

GUESS I'VE never been too worried about age. I've always looked a bit younger than I am. (Cool in your forties but pretty sucky at sixteen.)

I've watched people around me age fairly gracefully. My mum went grey very young, and I always thought she was STUNNING with her grey hair and ice blue eyes. I was always like, YUSS—I'm gonna be beautiful when I go grey!

I've also never been super athletic or active, so I've never given much thought to losing those things with age.

What I have lost though as each year goes by?

Fucks.

Many of them.

I just have fewer and fewer to give.

At thirty-eight, it started to dawn on me (and yes, I'm a bit slow): with age comes some COOL things.

Experience.

Insight.

Self-awareness.

CONFIDENCE in who and what I am *and am not.*

And so, at thirty-eight, I did the scariest thing I've ever done and started living my life differently than I knew my parents wanted. I left church. It had been my entire life experience, my entire world view. It influenced the clothes I put on each morning. The words that came out of my mouth. What I ate and drank. Who I spent time with. Where I would and wouldn't go. In our family, that had been *five generations* of history and belief and rules. And I was stepping out to break them all. Ouch.

Now, I need to put this in context: my parents ROCK. They are FREAKING AWESOME. They weren't oppressive or restrictive or judgemental of us growing up. They were (and still are) encouraging, accepting, loving, empowering. They are amazing examples of goodness.

So to go against the way they'd like me to live? Even at thirty-eight? That was terrifying. Not because of what they might think/say/do but because it would hurt them.

And who wants to hurt good parents?

But I decided this, with my newly unfurled, thirty-eight-year-old wings: I would rather live with the guilt of having hurt them than live feeling resentful toward them for what they wanted of me.

The things I started doing might seem trite, but in our context they're HUGE. I started drinking, swearing, wearing clothes that showed more and more of my skin to the world (and the sun, ahhhh), started having sex outside of marriage. I know, I'm boggling your mind because, like, seriously? For the first time? At thirty-eight-years old?

But think about it—those ways of living and seeing the world had been my *entire life experience.*

And so I need to tell you that this was a harder time in my life than when my husband left me. At twenty-three. With a one-year-old. AND THEN DROWNED.

I WOULD RATHER LIVE WITH THE GUILT OF HAVING HURT THEM THAN LIVE FEELING RESENTFUL TOWARD THEM FOR WHAT THEY WANTED OF ME.

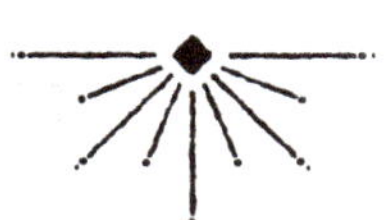

Come at me, world.   PHOTOGRAPHY BY SACHA

Me leaving church HURT.

AND we all survived it.

And I was better, stronger, more powerful in myself because of it.

And SO MANY women I know have a similar tale to tell. Not of leaving a religion, but of stripping away the weight of others' expectations. Peeling back those layers, often painfully, to discover what lies beneath.

And what lies beneath is glorious. And raw. And unfuckwithable.

This is what getting older has taught me: to live my truth.

YOU HAVE EVERY RIGHT TO BE RUDE

WAS SOOOOO RUDE to a telemarketer on the phone last night.

Carver Boy and I were sitting at our breakfast bar, having a quiet drink, and listening to *take me to bed* songs on YouTube. It's a relatively rare moment of beauty, and I neeeeeded it.

I saw an overseas number come up on my phone. I knew there was a good chance it would be one of those spammy, scammy calls, but I do work internationally, so I don't just ignore international numbers.

Kia ora, Shelly speaking, I said.

Hello Shelly, said a foreign accent, with the murmur of many voices in the background (both red flags), how are you?

And-BOOM-out-comes-no-more-fucks-to-give-Shelly-because-you-have-just-REACHED-INTO-MY-PRIVATE-SPACE-AND-MY-PER-SONAL-TIME-WITHOUT-PERMISSION.

I'll tell you how I am when you tell me who you are and what you want, I said.

I'm sorry? She said.

I'll tell you how I am, when you tell me who you are, and what you want. (Louder. Slower. Read the signs, bee-aahtch.)

Oh. OK. She said.

To be honest, I don't remember what she launched into next. But it was absolutely not, bottom-line-up-front, here's who I am and why I'm calling. It was a sales script.

I hung up.

Carver Boy looks at me.

Some scam, I say.

He nods, and we get back to our beautiful evening.

Maybe thirty minutes later, another number. Same country. This time, a man's voice. (Similar accent.)

Hello, he says, am I speaking to Shelly Davies?

Tell me who you are and what you want, I say. (Even less hesitation than last time—and there was VERY LITTLE hesitation last time, let me tell you. Now I'm just bordering on aggressive.)

Oh, OK, he says. I'm [insert name here] calling from Bla Bla Tech Company, he says—and he tries to keep talking, but I talk over the top of him.

What do you want? I say.

He starts to repeat himself and then you know what? The line goes dead!

WOO-FUCKING-HOO!!!

Carver boy is laughing by this stage. He still remembers *Demure Shelly* (maybe even misses her, ha ha). Watching me spread my wings is pretty much his 24/7 entertainment.

And by the way? I'd just like to salute the supervisor who was listening on that call and knew it was a waste of time to continue and HUNG UP ON ME. Now, that's a win.

So I started reflecting.

IT'S MY LIFE! I HAVE EVERY RIGHT TO PROTECT MYSELF IN ANY WAY I NEED TO, FROM ANYONE I FEEL THE NEED TO PROTECT MYSELF FROM.

Shelly-five-years-ago would never have behaved like that. Like, NEVER. She would never have been rude. EVER. Because all humans deserve respect.

I ABSOLUTELY STILL BELIEVE THAT!

My default position is to be loving and kind, no matter who you are. ALL HUMANS DESERVE RESPECT!

UNLESS.

They are imposing on you. Unless they are impinging on your rights. Unless they are pushing up against or crossing through your boundaries.

And I reflected on what has changed for me.

Because while Shelly-five-years-ago thought she wasn't ALLOWED to be rude, ever, that it was morally wrong, Shelly-in-her-forties has BOUNDARIES.

BOUNDARIES, BITCH!

Coz it's my right! It's my life! *I have every right* to protect myself in any way I need to, from anyone I feel the need to protect myself from.

IF WE WANT TO CHANGE OUR LIVES AND THE LIVES OF OUR CHILDREN, WE NEED TO QUESTION WHAT WE BRING INTO ADULTHOOD.

So many of us were raised before the age of consent. In days when you were forced to greet that uncle with a kiss, because #manners and #respectyourelders. We were raised with implicit messages that girls need to be nice. Polite. Compliant. Likeable. Don't upset people by having strong opinions (and voicing them, good lord).

But, my loves, if we want to change our lives and the lives of our children, we need to question what we bring into adulthood. Because not all of it should come.

For me, moving away from those societal expectations has been conscious and uncomfortable. I have voices inside me when I'm rude to a telemarketer that say, are you sure you needed to do that? Couldn't you have been a bit more polite? Did you need to be that aggressive? You used to be so much *nicer*.

Those voices make me ANGRY because I have to consciously listen to them so that I can reflect on where they're coming from, and why they're not speaking truth. It takes work, regular, conscious, consistent (#notmystrongsuit) work.

And those voices, just like these phone calls, which I get on a weekly, sometimes daily, basis, are from STRANGERS who HAVE NOT BEEN INVITED into my space.

I don't have to listen to them. I don't have to validate them. And I do NOT have to be polite to them.

They can fuck off.

That is all.

TO BECOME A ROCK STAR, BE A ROCKSTAR

WANT TO BE SOMETHING? Act like it.

I don't mean fake it till you make it, although there are elements of that in what I'm saying.

I guess I mean, if you want to be credible, speak credibly. If you want to be charismatic, step up your energy and engagement. If you want to be warm, act more warmly.

Don't wait to become something before you start acting like you are that something.

THAT'S NOT HOW IT WORKS.

It's like people who want to build a business before they start their business.

Yeah, nah.

I was with my clients Kathmandu in Christchurch late 2016. A year or so earlier, I had rebranded myself using my name, and got a website up and running that was bringing me in good leads and presenting me well.

But on this day, two separate people said to me, you need new photos on your website.

I had different hair, so fair enough.

But they said it was more than that.

We knew you were good at what you do, they said. *But we didn't know we were going to get THIS. You've got this rock star vibe. You perform. You enthral us.*

You need new pictures on your website.

Da-ham, I thought, and started thinking about what images would give a more rock star vibe. (P!nk, duh.) I also searched for a photographer that I thought could help me pull it off.

But as soon as I started getting the vision, I realized the bad news: these photos couldn't just be put on my current website. They were speaking my authentic voice in a way the current website wasn't.

I needed to build a new website. GAHDAMMIT!

I couldn't sleep.

I couldn't NOT do the thing I wanted to do: GO ALL OUT.

Be a Rockstar. Act like a Rockstar. Position myself like a Rockstar badass who knows her stuff and takes no shit and tells it like it is.

I called it my brand massacre.

I was terrified.

But *I couldn't not.*

And here we are. Shelly Davies, self-proclaimed Rockstar Writer-Trainer. Does a small part of me sometimes feel self-conscious about claiming that for myself? Yes. Does that tiny part sometimes worry what people will think? Yes. Because #human. But when people see my brand, my website, my email signature, do they know EXACTLY WHAT THEY'RE GONNA GET? Ohhh, fuck yes. And I've NEVER looked back.

So how do you want to be? And how would you act, show up, speak, *exist,* if you were already that?

Rockstars wear kick-ass heels and sit sideways on kick-ass chairs, right?
PHOTOGRAPHY BY SACHA

Are you waiting for something to happen first?

Don't wait.

Be.

Then become.

WHAT'S YOUR MOKO?

GREW UP HEARING STORIES of my Great-Great-Grandmother. Raihi Miraka Te Kewene Davies/Reweti Ngawaka. We knew her as Tupuna Raihi.

We heard stories of her as a leader, as strong, well-respected, loving, and generous above everything else.

We had one photo of her. And on her chin was a moko kauae—a traditional Māori chin tattoo. It's a sign of your identity, a celebration of your womanhood. A symbol of beauty and strength. She was the last in our family line to carry it before the introduction of Christianity discouraged the practice.

For me, she was like a princess with that marking on her chin. She was regal. I wanted to be like her. I wanted to be that beautiful, that proud, that strong. That courageous. That bold.

But.

We were religious. And tattoos of any kind were not an option for me, let alone a tattoo on my face.

WHAT IF YOU TURNED YOUR MAGIC ALL THE WAY THE FUCK ON?

—HADIIYAH BARBEL

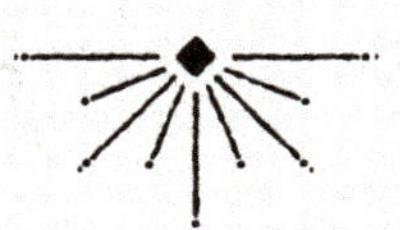

My great-great-grandmother, Tupuna Raihi. The last of our line to carry her moko kauae until me.
PHOTO TAKEN CIRCA 1925, PHOTOGRAPHER UNKNOWN.

It was simply an impossibility. A dream. Something to be wistfully wished for, not something that would ever happen.

In late 2017, as I continued to play with my unfurled wings and my new life away from the church, as I kept trying new things, leaning more into my whole self, kept peeling back the layers of things that had held me back, I felt a stirring within me for that tattoo. I started to reflect on my life and to ask myself, what if I could do it? What if it wasn't an impossibility?

What if.

I started to ask myself what was the worst that could happen if I got my moko kauae. There were two main answers:

1. My parents—I worried it would break their hearts. And,
2. People might question my right to wear it. People might judge me.

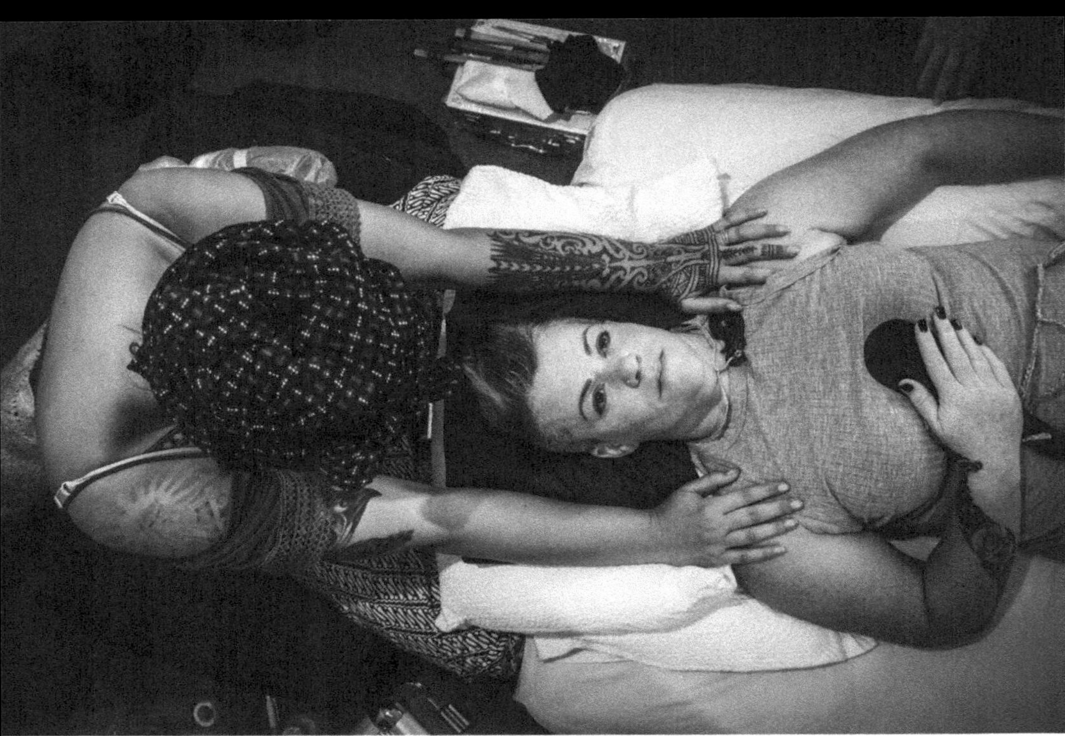

Pip Hartley (tā moko artist) preparing us before the work begins. Hamilton NZ April 2018.

OK, so fuck number two.

The only thing I was worried about was my parents. I didn't want to hurt them.

Hold that thought.

Then I asked myself, what was the best that could happen? And OMG so many more answers!

1. I would feel complete. It was the last thing I had wished for in my life but hadn't given myself permission to do—there would be no more *I wish I could*s left.
2. I would be proudly stating who I was, for all to see—my white skin wouldn't get in the way like it always had. There could be no more doubt who I am and where I come from.

3. I'd be an example for other Māori women who wanted this for themselves but needed courage.
4. I'd show my daughters that the world is theirs, to make of it what they wish.
5. I might feel even more bold, even more courageous, even more strong, with that mark on my chin, presenting me to the world. Claiming my right. Taking enough space in the world.

So I said it out loud:

I'm going to do this.

And once I said it, *it became true.*

I went and had the hard discussion with my parents. I listened to them. I took their advice. I acknowledged their worries.

They didn't die.

(Somewhere inside I had been terrified that this would be the last straw—I'd break their hearts. It'd kill them.)

The rest is history—you can *literally read it on my face.*

So my questions to you are:

What's YOUR moko?

What's your thing you wish you could do but think you can't?

What. If. You. Could?

What's the worst that could happen?

What's the best that could happen?

How do they balance out?

And now, what are you going to do about that?

Surrounded by women and family, Hamilton NZ April 2018.
PHOTOGRAPHY BY SACHA

Because, oh you gorgeous beings, we all have a moko inside of us. Something beautiful. Something stunningly, uniquely, truly, divinely you. An exquisite etching on your soul that both defines and emancipates you.

Loves, that etching is *crying out to see the light,* and no one can turn on the sun and the moon and the stars but you.

Ki te wheiao, ki te ao mārama.

Bring your moko into the light.

I know exactly who I am.

MY TEACHERS

Brené Brown, PhD, LMSW
Research professor,
University of Houston
www.brenebrown.com

**James Pope, MSocSci(Hons),
PGDipClinPsych, MNZCCP**
Clinical Psychologist
james@hsp.co.nz

Erika Napoletano, BATheatre
Writer of words, Teller of stories,
and all-round messy human
www.erikanapoletano.com

**Belinda Thomas BAPsych,
WTF, FU(Bitches)**
Performance Coach
www.performancehq.co.nz

Christina Marlett, BKin, BMT
Self-Care Coach
www.courageousself-care.com

Lynda Moore, GDA(Psych), BCOM
Money Mentalist
www.moneymentalist.com

**Jo Clarkson, MA,
 PGDipPsych(Clin)**
Clinical Psychologist
www.stressbox.co.nz

Kate Cherrington, MEd
Ngāti Hine
Puata Hou Ltd

Dione Davies, MA AT (Clinical)
Arts Therapist
www.aftertherain.co.nz

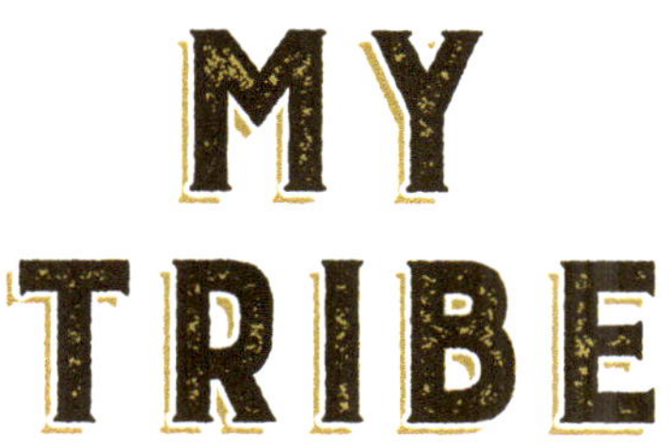

MY TRIBE

Michael Matchitt • Carver Boy • www.michaelmatchitt.com

Sacha Kahaki • Photography by Sacha • www.photosacha.com

Caylah Evans • Caylah Rose Creates • www.caylahrosecreates.com

Dani Simpson • Dynamic Media • www.dynamicmedia.co.nz

Jen W O'Deay • Feel These Words • www.feelthesewords.com

Jenna Heller • Author • www.authors.org.nz/author/jenna-heller

Sally Stephenson • Speculative Fiction Author • www.sastephenson.com

Davina Hughes • Genealogist, Writer, Print Manager

Ange King & Sara King • Playcentre Saviours & Soul Sisters

Victor Main • Writer & Entrepreneur

Mandy Smiler • Fairy God Ninja & Solicitor

ACKNOWLEDGEMENTS

To my Carver Boy Mike: I know you miss Demure Shelly some-times. But fuck, babe—look what the safety and reassurance of your hand on the small of my back has allowed me to become. Plus, #entertainmentvalue. Ko koe te tau o taku ate. I wouldn't be this me without you.

To my offspring, Lainn, Cody, Grace, and TheCrew: You have all been the greatest authors of my badassery. I'll forgive you for the excruciating pain in those lessons if you forgive me for all my years pre-badassery. Seeing you loving each other as adults and rocking your own worlds is a joy I simply never even knew was coming. E poho kererū ana au i a koutou.

To my parents and big sisters: Just love you. So. Much.

To the Unfuckwithable Girlfriends: you are my OG badasses!

To Lauren, SE, and the team at Lauren Taylor Shute Editorial: there's no one else I would ever entrust with my heart and soul embodied in print. Tēnā rawa atu koutou.

BIBLIOGRAPHY

Brown, Brené. *Daring greatly: How the Courage to Be Vulnerable Transforms the Way We Live, Love, Parent, and Lead.* New York, N.Y.: Gotham, 2012.

Brown, Brené. "Listening to Shame." Filmed March 2012 at TED, Long Beach, CA. Video, 20:22. www.ted.com/talks/brene_brown_listening_to_shame.

CliftonStrengths. "Home." Strengths Finder. Last modified July 13, 2021. www.gallup.com/cliftonstrengths/en/home.aspx

Napoletano, Erika. "Rethinking Unpopular." Filmed February 2012 at TEDxBoulder, Boulder, CO. Video, 16:54. www.tedxboulder.com/videos/rethinking-unpopular.

Young, J.E., Klosko, J.S., & Weishaar, M.E. *Schema Therapy: A Practitioner's Guide.* New York: Guilford Press, 2003.

SHELLY DAVIES has been described as the love-child of Brene Brown and P!nk—although her very awesome parents would probably disagree. She's of New Zealand Māori descent—a fact that is literally etched onto her chin—and she's known internationally for her unconventional and irresistible work in the field of plain language and clear communications.

At age thirty-seven, Shelly walked away from her family's five-generation commitment to a conservative Christian religion and started the exploratory period of her life, also known as "fucking shit up." She drank alcohol and coffee for the first time, started showing some skin to the daylight, and dedicated herself to fluency in a whole new language: profanity.

She now uses her hard-won lessons in badassery to inspire audiences around the globe to know themselves, love themselves, find power, and have joy. Shelly Davies lives in Rotorua, New Zealand with her Carver Boy, unless she's at home on Aotea, Great Barrier Island, not wearing pants.